# YOUR CHOICE

## A Personal Skills Course

# INTERPERSONAL COMMUNICATION
## Shay McConnon

MACMILLAN
EDUCATION

First published 1990
Reprinted 1990

Published by
MACMILLAN EDUCATION LTD
Houndmills, Basingstoke, Hampshire RG21 2XS
and London
Companies and representatives
throughout the world

Illustrated by Nick Oates and Bob Moulder

Printed in Hong Kong

British Library Cataloguing in Publication Data
McConnon, Shay
Interpersonal communication. – (Your choice)
1. Interpersonal relationships.
Communication
I. Title
302.2
ISBN 0–333–51118–2

# ■■■■■■■ CONTENTS ■■■■■■■

# ▬▬▬▬▬▬ INTRODUCTION ▬▬▬▬▬

Communication is a fundamental human skill and is the basis of all personal relationships. The quality of our interpersonal communication often determines the quality of these relationships.

There are two major aspects of communication: the ability to express oneself and the ability to listen. Communication problems are more often related to poor listening than to those of self-expression, hence there is an emphasis on listening in this course. It is viewed as an active rather than a passive activity, a skill which improves with practice and is essential to successful relationships.

This course recognises that the skills of interpersonal communication are not necessarily something we inherit or develop naturally but that they can and should be 'taught' and not left to be 'caught'.

This course offers a programme of structured experiences which aim to heighten awareness of and provide practice in the skills of interpersonal communication, together with opportunities for self-assessment and the identification of behaviour goals.

## Strategies 1–2

The opening strategies help students to an awareness of their own thoughts and feelings on interpersonal communication issues and to the idea that communication is a two-way process which requires both the speaker and the listener to be actively involved.

## Strategies 3–4

The role of body language is explored, its importance and the extent of its use. Students are encouraged to become more aware of their own non-verbal behaviours.

## Strategies 5–7

The skills of listening actively and reflectively in both verbal and non-verbal ways are identified and demonstrated. Students have the opportunity to practise these skills and receive feedback on their use.

## Strategies 8–9

Behaviours that hinder and block interpersonal communication are identified and students assess themselves on these.

## Strategies 10–11

Students assess themselves on the skills of communication that have been taught during the course. The assessment leads to an identification of behaviour goals and the opportunity for commitment to these goals using a structured plan for behaviour change.

## Strategies 12–13

The module concludes by recapping on the nature and practice of interpersonal communication and finally with an evaluation of the students' responses to this course.

## Appendix

The appendix offers some suggestions on using video during this course.

Most of the strategies involve small group work. The group can be the teacher's most effective resource in helping students to become aware of their ability to communicate effectively. The group also provides opportunities to experiment with new behaviours and receive feedback on them. Such work, however, requires sensitive handling by the teacher, who needs to create a positive, non-critical atmosphere in which individuals feel valued and listened to.

The time suggested for each strategy is an approximate guideline. The ability and maturity of the students will determine how long each strategy takes. Each strategy is divided into several phases which provide a natural break for limited time sessions. Most strategies include ideas for variations on the main procedure or a development of the exercise. Although the exercises are suitable across a wide age range, the teacher might wish to modify the content to make them more relevant to a specific group.

Recent initiatives in education encourage a move towards profiling, continuous assessment and reviewing. Assessment is to be seen as an integral part of all learning experiences. The student is at the centre of this process and its success requires that students understand the assessment procedure and are involved in the assessment process. Giving students a copy of their profile statements at the beginning of the course allows them to become aware of the assessment objectives. By explaining these objectives and the assessment procedure, students will know what to assess themselves on and how.

The review is a key element in effective profiling. Ideally this should take place at regular intervals during the course, rather than leaving the review to the end.

The students' completed worksheets could be used to form part of their formative profile and provide useful moments for reviewing with the student.

The teacher may wish to involve parents in this process and design the profile to allow them to make written comments.

The teacher could also design a scheme which asks students to assess themselves at the end of each session, e.g.

| | Sessions | | | | | | | |
|---|---|---|---|---|---|---|---|---|
| | 1 | 2 | 3 | 4 | 5 | 6 | 7 | 8 |
| **I work without supervision** | 8 | 6 | 7 | | | | | |
| **I work to the best of my ability** | 7 | 5 | | | | | | |
| **I am keen to learn** | 7 | 7 | | | | | | |

Students score themselves out of ten for each of these skill areas. Over a period of time, students will get a picture of themselves and be able to note areas of success along with skills needing attention. This can then be reviewed with the teacher.

However the profile is designed or executed, students hopefully will feel that their formative profiles are a tool they can use to become more aware of self, to monitor progress and then decide on new starting points.

The profile statement which follows is in two parts. (A) is an assessment sheet for skills taught during the course. (B) is an assessment sheet for students' attitudes and their ability to co-operate with each other. Each sheet allows both teacher and student to make independent comments on progress. These can be used as a basis for a review resulting in a joint comment.

# PROFILE STATEMENT (A): INTERPERSONAL COMMUNICATION

Name _____    Date _____

| | COMMENTS |
|---|---|
| 1 I can start a conversation with another person. | |
| 2 I know about body language. | |
| 3 I can use open-ended conversations to encourage others to talk. | |
| 4 I understand the skills of listening. | |
| 5 I can use these skills successfully. | |
| 6 I am aware of how people block communication. | |
| 7 I can assess my own interpersonal communication skills. | |
| 8 I can draw up a good plan to help me improve my communication skills. | |

## STUDENT

Report on the progress you have made:

## TEACHER

Report on this student's progress:

Signed _____ TEACHER

## JOINT COMMENTS

After discussion, we have agreed that progress has been made in:

But attention needs to be paid to:

The following action has been agreed on:

Signed _____ STUDENT

4

# PROFILE STATEMENT (B): INTERPERSONAL COMMUNICATION

Name _____ Date _____

## ATTITUDE AND WORKING WITH OTHERS

> Indicate your attitude marking the continuum line with an X.
> The teacher will score your attitude on this line with an O.

| | Always | | Sometimes | | Never |
|---|---|---|---|---|---|
| I work without supervision. | | | | | |
| I work to the best of my ability. | | | | | |
| I am keen to learn. | | | | | |
| I organise myself. | | | | | |
| I make good use of the time available. | | | | | |
| I co-operate with other students. | | | | | |
| I try to involve the quieter members. | | | | | |
| I make suggestions and offer ideas. | | | | | |
| I listen attentively to others. | | | | | |
| I help the group make decisions. | | | | | |
| I talk with confidence in the group. | | | | | |
| I try to understand other students' points of view. | | | | | |

**What I do well is:**

**What I could do better is:**

# MODULE OVERVIEW

| CHAPTER | DESCRIPTION | TYPE OF ACTIVITY | TIME | SIZE OF GROUP | WORK-SHEETS | ADDITIONAL MATERIALS | WORK EXTEN-SION |
|---|---|---|---|---|---|---|---|
| 1 This Is Me | Thoughts and feelings on a variety of communication issues are shared in small groups. | incomplete sentences | 30–40 | 4–6 | 1 | — | ✓ |
| 2 Are You Hearing Me? | Students are helped to appreciate that effective communication requires two people to be actively involved. | giving/receiving instructions | 30–40 | pairs | 2 | paper | ✓ |
| 3 My Body Talks! | The role of body language and the extent of its use in everyday communication is explored. | mime/interpretation | 30–40 | 5–6/pairs | 4 | — | ✓ |
| 4 Talking Gestures | Students are given opportunities to become aware of some of their non-verbal behaviours. | conditioned discussion | 30–40 | pairs/3 | — | — | ✓ |
| 5 I'm Listening | Non-verbal listening behaviours are demonstrated and students practise and are assessed in their use of these. | conversation/modelling | 60+ | pairs/3 or 4 | 2 | — | ✓ |
| 6 Keep Talking! | Attention is drawn to the use of open-ended questions and continuation expressions in listening effectively. | interviews/brainstorm | 60+ | 2–3/5–6/3 | 2 | paper, markers | ✓ |

# MODULE OVERVIEW

| CHAPTER | DESCRIPTION | TYPE OF ACTIVITY | TIME | SIZE OF GROUP | WORK-SHEETS | ADDITIONAL MATERIALS | WORK-EXTEN-SION |
|---|---|---|---|---|---|---|---|
| 7 I Hear You | Students are introduced to matching and paraphrasing, with opportunities to practise these. | mirroring/ paraphrasing | 30–40 | pairs/6–10 | — | — | ✓ |
| 8 Not Tuned In | Attention is drawn to behaviours, both verbal and non-verbal, that block communication. | role-play | 30–40 | pairs | 1 | — | ✓ |
| 9 Interference | Students assess themselves in the use of these blocking behaviours. | rank order/ assessment | 30–40 | pyramid groupings/ 4–6 | 2 | — | ✓ |
| 10 How Do I Rate? | Students are helped to an appraisal of their interpersonal communication skills. | assessment | 30–40 | pairs/6–8 | 2 | — | ✓ |
| 11 What Now? | Students identify target behaviours and commit themselves to these. | goal setting | 30–40 | varies/4–5 | 3 | completed observers' sheets | ✓ |
| 12 Game Talk | A card game which allows students to recap on the principles of good interpersonal communication. | card game | no fixed time | 5–6 | 5 | — | ✓ |
| 13 How Have We Got On? | An assessment of students' responses to these exercises. | evaluation | 30–40 | varies | 1 | — | ✓ |

## Aim:
To provide students with the opportunity to share thoughts and feelings on a variety of interpersonal communication issues.

## Procedure:

### • Phase I
○ Give each student the worksheet **THIS IS ME**.
○ Explain the task and give examples of completed sentences.
○ Allow time for students to complete the sentences.
○ Form groups of 4–6.
○ Students take it in turn to read out the first completed sentence. The others are to listen without making comments.
○ Students are free to pass.
○ The second sentence is shared with the group and the procedure continues as above.

### • Phase II
○ Reconvene the class and invite students to comment on what they have learned from each other:
  – How do they generally feel when they are interrupted?
  – How do they feel when people listen to them?
  – What do they feel about those who give put-downs? . . . and so on

## Extensions:
1 Turn this into a game. Transfer the incomplete sentences on to cards. Divide the class into groups of 4–6. Shuffle the cards. In turn, each student takes a card and completes the sentence. Students are free to pass or delay responding, allowing them time to give a satisfactory response.
2 The class forms two circles, an inner and an outer circle, with students facing each other in pairs. Read aloud one of the incomplete sentences. Each student completes it with his partner. Continue for three sentences and then one circle moves to the left. Read out another three sentence stems and continue with the above procedure.

**Group Size:** 4–6

**Time:** 30–40 minutes

**Materials:** Each student requires:
○ worksheet **THIS IS ME**

## Notes:
This opening strategy helps students to an awareness of their own thoughts and feelings on interpersonal communication issues. Students are asked to complete sentences which relate to the topic and then share these in small groups. Students are free to answer at whatever level they choose.

This strategy can be used as a written homework assignment or as a stimulus for discussion work. It can be used at any stage during the course.

One way of using the strategy over several sessions is to group the incomplete sentences in blocks of five and ask the class to complete them at the beginning or end of a session.

# THIS IS ME

Name _____   Date _____

1  When someone interrupts me I _____

2  When someone stares at me I _____

3  When someone listens to me I _____

4  With someone who is quiet and shy I _____

5  With someone who talks a lot I _____


6  When talking to someone who fidgets a lot I _____
_____

7  The people I find it easy to speak to are _____

8  When I run out of things to say I _____

9  When talking to someone who doesn't look at me I _____
_____

10  When I speak in front of a group of people I _____
_____


11  The people I find it difficult to speak to are _____
_____

12  When someone doesn't listen to me I _____

13  When someone talks about themselves all the time I _____
_____

14  The way I am dressed probably says _____

15  When someone gives me a put-down I _____


16  With someone who is noisy and loud I _____

17  When someone ignores me I _____

18  With strangers I _____

19  When someone keeps on offering me advice I _____
_____

20  I find it difficult to speak when _____

# 2 ARE YOU HEARING ME? ■■■■■

**Aim:** To demonstrate that effective communication is a two-way process requiring both speaker and listener to be actively involved.

## Procedure:

### • Phase I
○ Form pairs with students sitting facing each other.
○ Students talk to each other simultaneously about: 'Everything I did since getting up this morning'.
○ Each student is to concentrate on her story and should keep talking all the time.
○ Continue for about one minute.
○ Reconvene the class and invite comments on the following:
  – What was happening between the two speakers?
  – Were they communicating?
  – Why? Why not?
  – How could communication improve?

### • Phase II
○ Regroup to pairs and decide who is to be A and B.
○ Give A the worksheet **ONE-WAY COMMUNICATION (A)** and give B a sheet of plain paper.
○ Students are to sit back to back so that the drawing on the worksheet is not seen by B.
○ A now describes the drawing on the worksheet so that B can produce an identical copy on her sheet of paper.
○ *B is not allowed to ask any questions.*
○ When complete, students compare drawings and note the variations.
○ Swap roles and use the worksheet **ONE-WAY COMMUNICATION (B)**.
○ Every student should now have experienced both roles.
○ Discuss the experience with the class:
  – Who found it easy?
  – Who found it difficult? Why?
  – How did the speaker feel? (frustrated, confused, angry?)
  – How did the listener feel? (frustrated, confused, angry?)
  – Were there many variations between the finished and original drawings?
  – What does this say about the communication?
  – How could communication be more effective?

### • Phase III
○ Repeat the procedure of Phase II using the worksheet **TWO-WAY COMMUNICATION (A)** and **(B)**, only this time questions may be asked.

**Group Size:** Pairs

**Time:** 30–40 minutes

**Materials:** Each pair requires:
○ worksheet **ONE-WAY COMMUNICATION (A)** and **(B)** (cut into two)
○ worksheet **TWO-WAY COMMUNICATION (A)** and **(B)** (cut into two)
○ 4 sheets of plain paper

## Notes:

Young people are not always aware of the complexity of interpersonal communication. It is not simply 'talking' to the other person but also requires that people listen carefully and check that they have heard correctly.

This strategy introduces students to the idea of communication as a two-way process which requires both speaker and listener to be actively involved. Phase I, which involves all students talking simultaneously, can become noisy and the teacher may prefer instead to ask a couple of volunteers to demonstrate 'talking each other down' in front of the class.

Phase II should illustrate that one-way communication (i.e. when only one person speaks) is limited and the teacher can draw attention to the variations between the finished and original drawings as evidence for this.

Students are allowed to question their partners in Phase III and this should result in greater accuracy between the finished and original drawings demonstrating the importance of listening and checking out to effective communication.

This exercise can be adapted in a variety of ways, e.g. with student A constructing a shape out of lego and B attempting to reproduce this.

○ Discuss the experience with the class:
  – How did the speaker feel this time?
  – How did the listener feel now that she was able to check out what was being said?
  – Was there greater accuracy in the reproduction of the drawings?
  – Was communication more effective? Why?

## Extensions:

1 A volunteer stands with her back to the class and describes a picture she has drawn (composed of some geometric shapes) using words only. The class reproduce this on paper as best they can. Compare the drawings. Repeat this, but with the volunteer facing the class and using her hands as well as words. Finally, the volunteer faces the class, describes the picture and answers questions from the students.

2 Form groups of 6–8. Out of sight of the other students show one member of the group one of the drawings from the worksheets for 20 seconds. She is given one minute to reproduce it. This reproduction is now shown to another student for 20 seconds and she has to reproduce that drawing in one minute. Continue with the other group members. No student should see any drawing except that made by the preceding person. At the end, compare all the drawings with the original.

3 Form a circle of 10–15. Whisper a message to one student, who whispers it to the next, and so on until it reaches the original student. Compare the two messages. This can be varied by having two messages going round the circle simultaneously in different directions.

# ONE-WAY COMMUNICATION (A)

Describe clearly this series of shapes.
You may repeat your instructions a second time.
You are not allowed to answer any questions.

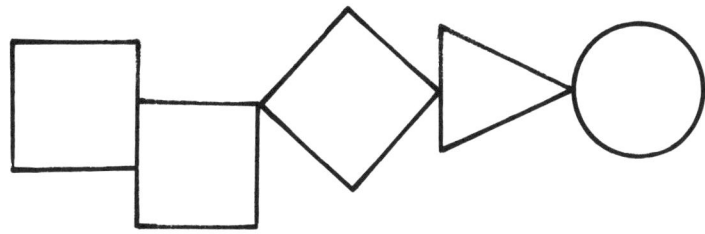

# ONE-WAY COMMUNICATION (B)

Describe clearly this series of shapes.
You may repeat your instructions a second time.
You are not allowed to answer any questions.

# TWO-WAY COMMUNICATION (A)

Describe clearly this series of shapes.
You may repeat your instructions a second time.
You are allowed to answer questions.

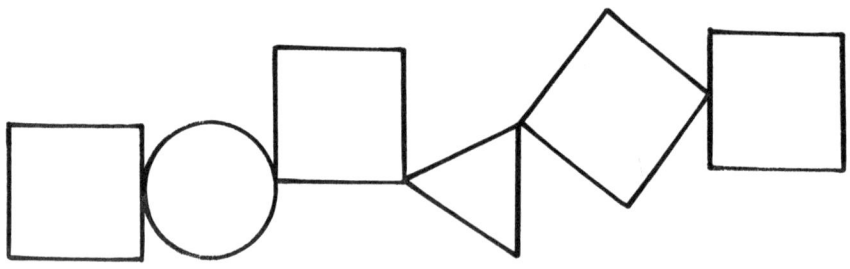

# TWO-WAY COMMUNICATION (B)

Describe clearly this series of shapes.
You may repeat your instructions a second time.
You are allowed to answer questions.

## Procedure:

- **Phase I**
  ○ Form groups of 5–6.
  ○ Give each group a set of **EMOTION CARDS**. These are shuffled and placed face down.
  ○ A volunteer selects a card and then tries to communicate this emotion non-verbally to the other group members.
  ○ The other group members have to guess the emotion.
  ○ Students take it in turn to select a card and convey an emotion.

- **Phase II**
  ○ In the same groups, a volunteer again selects an emotion card.
  ○ This student speaks a nursery ryhme (e.g. Mary had a little lamb) in a tone of voice that conveys that emotion.
  ○ The group has to guess the emotion.
  ○ Students take it in turn to do this.

- **Phase III**
  ○ Give each student the worksheet **(A) WHAT ARE THEY SAYING?**
  ○ In pairs, students complete their worksheets.
  ○ Reconvene the class and invite students to report on their interpretations.

- **Phase IV**
  ○ Give each student the worksheet **(B) WHAT ARE THEY SAYING?**
  ○ Explain the task.
  ○ In pairs, students complete their worksheets.
  ○ Form groups of 6 and share interpretations.
  ○ Reconvene the class and read aloud the **ANSWER SHEET**.
  ○ Discuss:
    – Who found it easy?
    – Who found it difficult?
    – Were many correct in their interpretations?
    – How much do we communicate in non-verbal ways?
    – Is it a language we can learn to use as we do with spoken language?

### Extensions:
1 In groups of 5–6 a volunteer selects an emotion card and then 'sculpts' another student's body to convey this emotion. The other group members have to guess the emotion. Students take it in turn to 'sculpt' and be 'sculpted'.
2 The teacher calls out an emotion and the students assume a body position which signals that emotion.

**Group Size:** 5–6; pairs

**Time:** 30–40 minutes

**Materials:** Each group requires:
○ set of **EMOTION CARDS**

Each student requires:
○ worksheet **(A) WHAT ARE THEY SAYING?**
○ worksheet **(B) WHAT ARE THEY SAYING?**

The teacher requires:
○ worksheet **ANSWER SHEET**

## Notes:
When we communicate we use not only our voices but also our bodies. Experts say that 70 to 80 per cent of our communication with others is non-verbal, i.e. facial expressions, body posture, gestures, tone of voice, mannerisms, and so on.

This strategy introduces students to body language and its role in communication. Phases I and II require students to use body language to communicate emotions and the remaining Phases involve students interpreting non-verbal signals.

Some emotions can be difficult to communicate and the teacher may wish to limit the emotion cards for Phases I and II to those which are easily distinguishable in non-verbal terms.

A homework assignment can be given asking students to each take a different emotion and make a collage using pictures from magazines, newspapers, comics etc. showing how this emotion can be communicated in various non-verbal ways.

3 Play a TV programme with the sound turned down. Students are to pick up clues as to what is happening and being said from hand movements, facial expressions, body positions etc. and then discuss their interpretations.
4 Give students headbands on which are written various personality traits, e.g. I'M A BULLY, I'M BORING etc. The person wearing the headband must not know what is written on it. Students wander around the room in silence and react non-verbally to each other's headbands. Students are to guess from these reactions what the label says.

# EMOTION CARDS

| | | | |
|---|---|---|---|
| CONFUSED | REJECTED | WORRIED | NERVOUS |
| ASHAMED | DEPRESSED | STUBBORN | SHY |
| SAD | EXCITED | SURPRISED | EMOTIONLESS |
| SCARED | HAPPY | BORED | ANGRY |

# (A) WHAT ARE THEY SAYING?

Name _____

Date _____

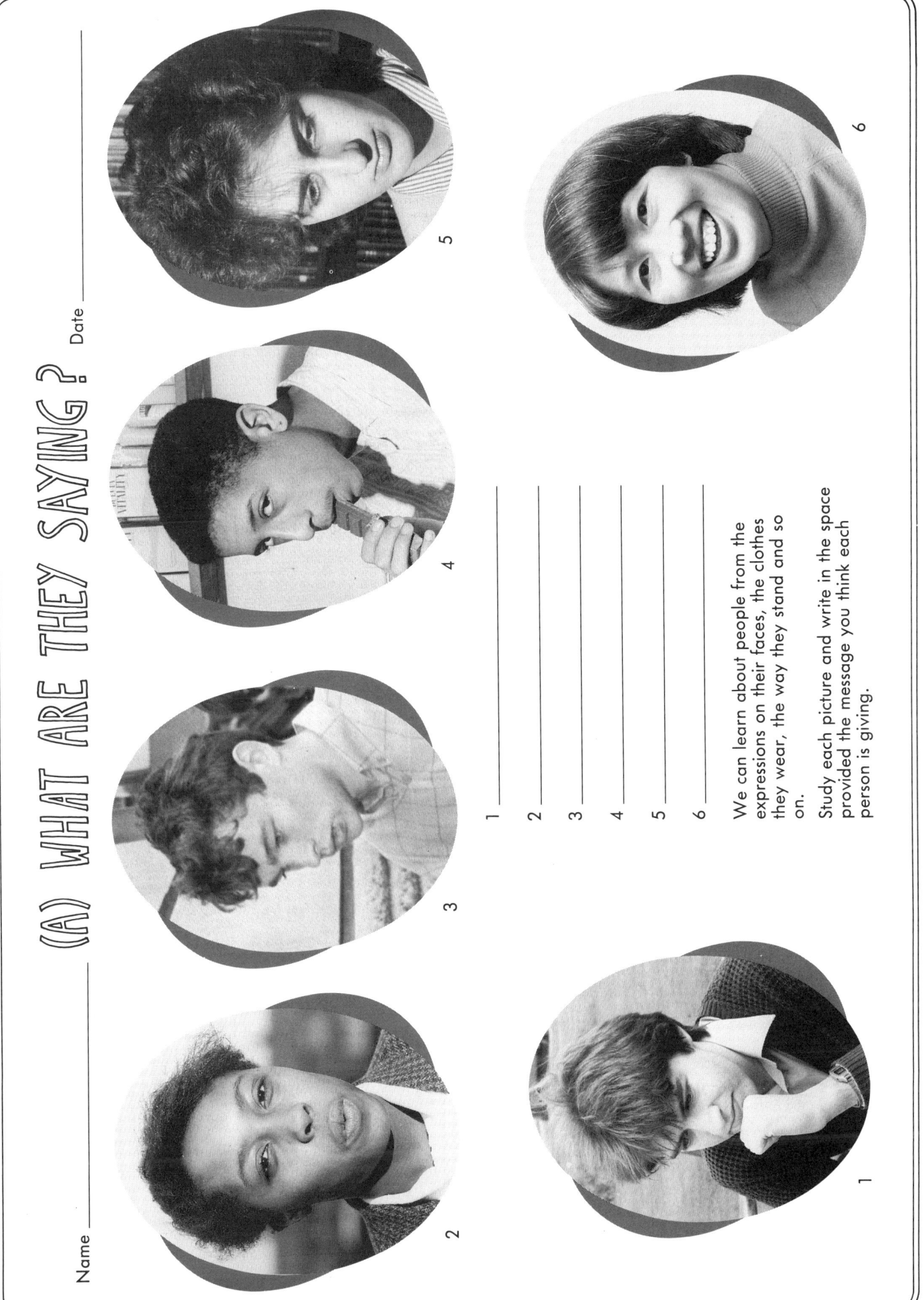

We can learn about people from the expressions on their faces, the clothes they wear, the way they stand and so on.

Study each picture and write in the space provided the message you think each person is giving.

1 _____

2 _____

3 _____

4 _____

5 _____

6 _____

17

# (B) WHAT ARE THEY SAYING?

Using body language clues, decide what the characters in this strip are saying and then fill in the bubbles.

18

# ANSWER SHEET

**Aim:** To help students to an awareness of some of their non-verbal behaviours.

# Procedure:

- **Phase I**
- ○ Form pairs.
- ○ Students sit back to back and begin a conversation about 'The food I like'.
- ○ Continue for one minute.
- ○ Pairs next sit facing each other and carry out a conversation, but with eyes closed, about 'My favourite TV programmes'.
- ○ Continue for one minute.
- ○ Pairs sit facing each other and carry out a conversation, but sitting on their hands, about 'The clothes I like to wear'.
- ○ Continue for one minute.
- ○ Pairs pretend to be both deaf and dumb.
- ○ They are to plan a summer holiday together but can only communicate by mime.

- **Phase II**
- ○ Reconvene the class and invite comments on the experience:
  - – How did students feel when they had no eye contact?
  - – When they could not use their hands?
  - – When they could not speak?
  - – How important are eye contact, gestures and facial expressions to communication?
  - – Do we need to pay close attention to these non-verbal ways of communicating? Why?

- **Phase III**
- ○ Form groups of 3 and decide who is to be A, B and C.
- ○ A and B carry out a conversation about 'When I leave school'.
- ○ C observes A's body language.
- ○ Allow the conversation to continue for 1–2 minutes.
- ○ C now feeds back her observations to A.
- ○ Repeat this procedure until everyone has played all three roles.

- **Phase IV**
- ○ Students regroup to pairs and decide who is to be A and B.
- ○ Pairs stand facing each other about 6–8 feet apart.
- ○ A remains stationary.
- ○ B walks slowly towards A.
- ○ A calls 'Stop' when she starts to feel uncomfortable, i.e. when B starts to get too close.
- ○ Students note the distance between them.
- ○ Reconvene the class tand discuss:
  - – How did students feel doing this exercise?
  - – Did some pairs get closer than others?
  - – Why might this be?

**Group Size:** Pairs then groups of 3

**Time:** 30–40 minutes

**Materials:** None

## Notes:

Having explored the role of body language in the previous strategy, students are now given an opportunity to become aware of some of their own non-verbal behaviours.

The session opens with students taking part in several communication exercises in which they are restricted in their use of non-verbal behaviours (e.g. no eye contact, no hand movements). In this way it is hoped to sharpen the students' awareness of their use of these behaviours. Phase III provides opportunities for students to be observed and receive feedback on their use of body language.

Alternative conversation topics: 'If I were a millionaire', 'My family', 'If I had three wishes', 'School meals', 'My favourite hobby'.

Young people are not always aware of the concept of personal space, i.e. the distance we like to keep between ourselves and others, and Phase IV should help students who have difficulties with this.

Encourage students to become aware of the non-verbal messages they give in everyday situations: talking to a friend, using the telephone, at the meal table, and so on.

- – How do students feel when someone gets too close?
- – How would you know if you are too close to a person?
- – Any tips/suggestions for people who are inclined to get too close?

## Extensions:

1 Groups of 5–6 sit in a circle, chairs facing outwards. They then carry out a discussion with their backs to each other.

2 Invite two students at a time to the front of the class. A stands with hands behind back. B stands immediately behind A and puts her hands forward so that they appear to belong to A. A begins talking and B supplies the hand movements.

3 Invite a volunteer to speak to the class, without hand movements, about baking a cake, changing a plug etc.

**Aim:** To help students become aware of non-verbal listening behaviours, to practise these and be assessed in their use.

# Procedure:

## • Phase I
○ Form pairs and decide who is to be A and B.
○ Give A an instruction card, the details of which remain secret from B.
○ B begins a conversation on 'What I like about school'.
○ A responds according to his secret instruction.
○ Allow 1–2 minutes for the conversation.
○ B now guesses what the instruction was on A's card.
○ Give B a card.
○ Reverse roles and B responds according to the instructions on his card.
○ Continue this procedure with different cards until each student has experienced a variety of listening and non-listening situations.

## • Phase II
○ Reconvene the class and invite students to comment on the experience:
  – How did it feel when they weren't listened to?
  – How did it feel when they were listened to?
  – How did it feel when they weren't listening to their partner?
  – How did it feel when they listened to their partner?
  – What happens when people don't listen to each other?/When people do listen to each other?
  – Which is more important – listening or talking?

## • Phase III
○ Invite students to give examples of good non-verbal listening behaviours.
○ Demonstrate with the help of a student a variety of these listening behaviours e.g. eye contact, leaning forward, relaxed body pose, head nodding.
○ Form groups of 3 (or 4) and students decide who is to be A, B and C.
  – A is the speaker.
  – B is the listener.
  – C is the observer (the observer's role could be divided between two students – see Notes).
○ Give the observer's sheet **NON-VERBAL BEHAVIOURS** to C (cut into two if there are two observers).
○ Draw attention to the behaviours to be observed and explain how the sheet is to be completed (see Notes).

**Group Size:** Pairs then groups of 3 or 4

**Time:** 60+ minutes

**Materials:** Each student requires:
○ observer's sheet **NON-VERBAL BEHAVIOURS**

The teacher requires:
○ set of **SECRET INSTRUCTION CARDS**

○ A begins a conversation on 'What I dislike about school'.
○ B is to join in the conversation and demonstrate good non-verbal listening behaviours.
○ C is to observe B and complete the observer's sheet.
○ After 2–3 minutes swap roles.
○ When each has had the opportunity to be speaker, listener and observer, students complete the rest of the observer's sheet.
○ Cs now take it in turn to give feedback on what they observed, commenting on what the student did well and also drawing attention to skills requiring attention.
○ Reconvene the class and recap on non-verbal listening behaviours.

## Extensions:
1 In pairs, students sit facing each other and take it in turn to share an observation about their partners. The observation may relate to posture, facial expression, tone of voice etc., e.g.
   A: I notice that you are leaning slightly towards me.
   B: I notice that your arms are folded.
2 In groups of 5–6, students brainstorm for listening and non-listening behaviours. Each group is to report back and the teacher draws up a list of listening and non-listening behaviours on the board. Students could rank order the two lists.
3 In pairs, students 'sculpt' their partner into a communication pose that looks relaxed and confident. They check this out with their partner and if necessary their partner makes adjustments to this pose.

# Notes:

This strategy continues to focus on body language and looks specifically at listening behaviours. It is the first of several strategies that cover listening, and provides students with the opportunity to experience a variety of listening and non-listening behaviours. Non-verbal listening behaviours are demonstrated and students have the opportunity to practise and be assessed in their use of these.

Listening is a critical part of the communication process. It is to be considered an active rather than a passive activity. It is a skill which is complex and one which improves with practice. Young people are not always aware of its importance to relationships nor view it as a skill to be practised.

We show we are interested, attentive and listening through:

*Posture*: A relaxed body posture puts the speaker at ease. A slight lean forward shows interest and that the listener's focus is on the speaker.

*Voice*: The volume, tone and pace of a person's voice can be used to convey feelings and interest. The listener's feelings should reflect those of the speaker. To reply with a happy sounding voice is inappropriate when the speaker is sad.

*Eye contact*: Good eye contact shows you are aware of the speaker, interested and listening. A stare can threaten, and looking down or away can be interpreted as disinterest or boredom. Eye contact is also important as it allows you to be aware of the speaker's non-verbal messages.

*Facial expression*: A listening expression is relaxed and friendly. Smiling may suggest that you are open and friendly. Facial expression should match the speaker's emotion, e.g. to grin as the speaker shows sadness indicates that you are not 'in tune' with him.

*Gestures*: The use of hands and arms can add 'colour' and emphasis to what the speaker is saying. Too many or exaggerated gestures can indicate a person is nervous.

*Spatial distance*: People's feelings towards each other can be communicated by physical proximity. Generally, the friendlier you are the closer you get. People feel uncomfortable when their personal space is encroached.

*Head movements*: The use of head nods is particularly important in listening. It signifies that you are interested, paying attention and encouraging the speaker to continue.

*Fiddling movements*: Fidgeting indicates nervousness, disinterest or boredom.

In Phase III you may prefer to choose two observers rather than one. The observer's sheet **NON-VERBAL BEHAVIOURS** is designed so that, if necessary, it can be cut into two. Draw attention to the behaviours to be observed and how the sheet is to be completed. As an example to the class, you could invite two volunteers to carry out a conversation while you complete an observer's sheet.

A video recorder could be used to heighten the students' awareness of themselves and their listening behaviours. It would be useful to record Phase III and, during playback, attention could be drawn to the good use of listening skills.

Alternative conversation topics: 'The people I like', 'My life in ten years' time', 'I am happy when . . .', 'If I had £100', 'If I had three wishes', 'The people I dislike'.

# SECRET INSTRUCTION CARDS

Take part in the conversation and *SMILE AND BE INTERESTED.*

Take part in the conversation and *NOD YOUR HEAD* to encourage your partner to speak.

Take part in the conversation and *LEAN SLIGHTLY TOWARDS THE SPEAKER.*

Take part in the conversation and *MIRROR THE SPEAKER'S BODY LANGUAGE.*

Take part in the conversation but *FIDGET WITH YOUR CLOTHES.*

Take part in the conversation but *KEEP A BLANK EXPRESSION.*

Take part in the conversation but *KEEP SCRATCHING YOUR NOSE.*

Take part in the conversation and *KEEP GOOD EYE CONTACT* with your partner.

Take part in the conversation but *STARE AT THE SPEAKER.*

Take part in the conversation but *LEAN FAR BACK.*

Take part in the conversation but *KEEP LOOKING AT YOUR WATCH.*

Take part in the conversation but *KEEP TUGGING YOUR EAR.*

Take part in the conversation but *DON'T LOOK AT THE SPEAKER'S EYES.*

Listen quietly to your partner but *SAY NOTHING.*

Take part in the conversation but *TURN SIDEWAYS TO THE SPEAKER.*

Take part in the conversation but *YAWN A LOT.*

# NON-VERBAL BEHAVIOURS

Name _____

Observed by _____

Date _____

CIRCLE THOSE BEHAVIOURS YOU OBSERVE.

| GESTURES | A lot/some/none. Smooth/jerky. Exaggerated/microscopic. |
|---|---|
| FACIAL EXPRESSION | Relaxed/tense. Smile/frown/blank. Changes with speaker's expression. |
| HEAD MOVEMENTS | A lot/some/none. |
| FIDDLING MOVEMENTS | A lot/some/none. Fidgeting/scratching/leg swinging/shifting position. |

_____ COMMUNICATES WELL

BECAUSE _____

_____ WOULD COMMUNICATE BETTER IF S/HE

_____

# NON-VERBAL BEHAVIOURS

Name _____

Observed by _____

Date _____

CIRCLE THOSE BEHAVIOURS YOU OBSERVE.

| POSTURE | Leans forward/leans back. Slouches/upright. Relaxed/tense. |
|---|---|
| VOICE | Loud/quiet. Fast/slow. Monotonous/interesting. Mumbled/clear. |
| EYE CONTACT | A lot/some/none. Appeared to stare/ looked and looked away comfortably. |
| SPATIAL DISTANCE | Close/far away/just right. Partner appeared comfortable/uncomfortable. |

_____ COMMUNICATES WELL

BECAUSE _____

_____ WOULD COMMUNICATE BETTER IF S/HE

_____

24

## Aim:
To introduce students to open-ended questions and continuation expressions, with an opportunity to practise and be assessed in the use of these.

# Procedure:

- ### Phase I
  ○ Form groups of 2–3 and give each student the worksheet **INTERVIEW**.
  ○ Each group is to devise a questionnaire to find out as much as possible about another person.
  ○ The questionnaire is to comprise 10 questions:
    − 5 questions are to be phrased so that they receive a YES/NO answer.
    − 5 questions are to be open-ended, i.e. to receive an answer of more than one word.
  ○ When complete, students interview a person of their choice using this questionnaire.
  ○ Questions and answers are to be recorded on the worksheet.

- ### Phase II
  ○ Reconvene the class and discuss:
    − Which type of questions were easiest to design, open or closed?
    − Which type of questions gave the interviewer most information?
    − Why is this?
    − What kind of words do open-ended questions usually begin with?
    − Would these type of questions indicate interest and listening? Why?

- ### Phase III
  ○ Form groups of 5–6.
  ○ Give paper and a marker to each group.
  ○ Each group chooses a secretary and a spokesperson.
  ○ Each group brainstorms for words and phrases that indicate interest and listening, i.e. that encourage the other person to continue talking.
  ○ The secretary notes these on the paper.
  ○ Allow 5–6 minutes for the brainstorm.
  ○ Each group now stars the three most helpful words or phrases for showing interest and listening.
  ○ Reconvene the class and invite groups to report back.
  ○ Make a list of the helpful words and phrases on the blackboard/flipchart.
  ○ Add to this list if necessary (see Notes) and draw attention to the use of continuation expressions during pauses and moments of hesitation, such as 'I see', 'Mm'.
  ○ Students now complete the WORDS FOR LISTENING box on the worksheet, making a selection from the blackboard or brainstorm.

**Group Size:** 2–3; 5–6; 3

**Time:** 60 + minutes

**Materials:** Each group requires:
○ paper and marker

Each student requires:
○ worksheet **INTERVIEW**
○ observer's sheet **VERBAL BEHAVIOURS**

## Notes:

This strategy looks at another aspect of listening actively − the use of open-ended questions and continuation expressions.

A closed question tends to invite a 'yes' or 'no' answer, e.g. 'Do you like watching TV?' Whereas open-ended questions, which are less restricting, generally allow a conversation to run more fluently, e.g. 'What TV programmes do you like?' Open-ended questions begin with words like 'What', 'How', 'When', 'Where' and 'Could'.

'Continuation expressions' are signals of encouragement which can be used during pauses and moments of hesitation, e.g. 'I see', 'Really?' 'Mm', 'Aha', 'Oh', 'Go on', 'Interesting', 'Yes', 'When?' 'And?' 'So' etc.

Phase III requires students to draw up a list of words and phrases which invite and encourage a speaker to continue talking. These will be useful for young people to have in their repertoire of communication skills.

A video recorder can be used to heighten the students' awareness of their listening behaviours. Phase IV would be useful to record. During playback, attention can be drawn to the good use of listening skills.

- ### Phase IV
  ○ Form groups of 3.
  ○ Explain that each student will have the opportunity to host her own chat show.
  ○ Students decide who is to be A, B and C and what they would like to be interviewed about.
    − A is the chat show host.
    − B is the guest to be interviewed.
    − C is the observer.

○ Give the observer's sheet **VERBAL BEHAVIOURS** to C.
○ Draw attention to the behaviours to be observed and explain how the sheet is to be completed.
○ The chat show now begins.
○ Allow 3–5 minutes for the interview.
○ Swap roles allowing each student to be the host, guest and observer.
○ After the interviews, allow time for students to complete any unfinished sections of the observer's sheet.
○ Cs now give feedback on what they observed.
○ Reconvene the class and discuss:
  – How did students feel being the host?
  – How did students feel being the guest?
  – Was it easy or difficult?
  – What techniques did the hosts find helpful?

## Extensions:

1 Students write the names of famous people (real or fictional) on slips of paper. These are to be pinned to the backs of everyone in the group without them seeing the person's name. Each student has to find out what the name on her back is by asking the other students questions about the person's background or characteristics. This activity can be used as an opportunity for students to ask open and closed questions and compare their usefulness.

2 In some contexts, Phase IV will work better if two people act as chat show hosts encouraging the guest to speak. This lessens the pressure on one person being responsible for asking open-ended questions and using continuation expressions.

3 Make a list of closed questions, e.g. 'Do you like school?' which the students have to rewrite as open-ended questions, e.g. 'How are you getting on at school?'

# INTERVIEW

Design a questionnaire to find out as much as possible about another person.
5 questions are to be phrased so that they receive a YES/NO answer.
5 questions are to be phrased so that they receive an answer of more than one word.
In small groups, design your questionnaire and write the questions in the left-hand box.
Interview a person of your choice and record their answers in the right-hand box.

## AN INTERVIEW WITH

_____

### YES/NO QUESTIONS

1 ....................................................
2 ....................................................
3 ....................................................
4 ....................................................
5 ....................................................

### OPEN-ENDED QUESTIONS

1 ....................................................
....................................................
....................................................
2 ....................................................
....................................................
....................................................
3 ....................................................
....................................................
....................................................
4 ....................................................
....................................................
....................................................
5 ....................................................
....................................................
....................................................

### WORDS FOR LISTENING

1 ....................................................
2 ....................................................
3 ....................................................
4 ....................................................
5 ....................................................
6 ....................................................

### ANSWERS

1 ....................................................
2 ....................................................
3 ....................................................
4 ....................................................
5 ....................................................

### ANSWERS

1 ....................................................
....................................................
....................................................
....................................................
2 ....................................................
....................................................
....................................................
....................................................
3 ....................................................
....................................................
....................................................
....................................................
4 ....................................................
....................................................
....................................................
....................................................
5 ....................................................
....................................................
....................................................

# VERBAL BEHAVIOURS

Name _____

Observed by _____

Date _____

CIRCLE THOSE BEHAVIOURS YOU OBSERVE.

| VERBAL FOLLOWING | Stays on subject/digresses. |
|---|---|
| QUESTIONS | A lot/some/none. Open-ended/closed. |
| CONTINUATION EXPRESSIONS | A lot/some/none. |

_____ COMMUNICATES WELL

BECAUSE _____

_____ WOULD COMMUNICATE BETTER IF S/HE

_____

---

# VERBAL BEHAVIOURS

Name _____

Observed by _____

Date _____

CIRCLE THOSE BEHAVIOURS YOU OBSERVE.

| VERBAL FOLLOWING | Stays on subject/digresses. |
|---|---|
| QUESTIONS | A lot/some/none. Open-ended/closed. |
| CONTINUATION EXPRESSIONS | A lot/some/none. |

_____ COMMUNICATES WELL

BECAUSE _____

_____ WOULD COMMUNICATE BETTER IF S/HE

_____

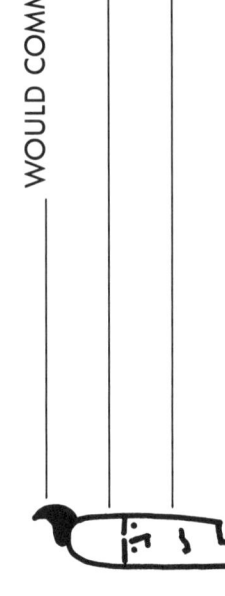

28

**Aim:** To draw attention to the importance of matching and paraphrasing to communication and provide students with the opportunity to practise these.

# Procedure:

## • Phase I
○ In pairs, students stand facing each other, shoulder-width apart.
○ One student moves his hands and the other attempts to mirror this movement.
○ Students are to maintain eye contact for this activity.
○ After two minutes, swap roles.
○ Repeat with a different activity using other body parts (e.g. legs) and changing the pace of the movement.

## • Phase II
○ Form pairs and students decide who is to be A and B.
○ A talks about what he did over the weekend.
○ B is to join in the conversation and mirror A's non-verbal behaviours.
○ After two minutes swap roles.
○ Reconvene the class and discuss:
  – Did students find it easy or difficult to match their partner's behaviour?
  – Did matching affect the conversation? How?
  – Could matching give people the feeling of being listened to?

## • Phase III
○ Groups of 6–10 form a circle.
○ Give each group member a number.
○ A volunteer makes up the first sentence of a story and calls out a number.
○ The group member with that number paraphrases what has been said, adds another sentence and calls out a different number.
○ Continue for 5–6 minutes.

## • Phase IV
○ The class forms two circles, an inner and an outer circle, with students facing each other in pairs.
○ The inner circle of students start to talk about: 'My life would be better if . . .'.
○ Their partners join in the conversation but must first paraphrase what the other student has said to that student's satisfaction.
○ Continue for 3–5 minutes with both students paraphrasing what each has just said before contributing to the conversation.
○ The inner circle moves two places to the left.
○ The outer circle of students speak to their new partners on 'My life in ten years' time'.

**Group Size:** Pairs; 6–10
**Time:** 30–40 minutes
**Materials:** None

○ Again the paraphrasing rule applies.
○ Reconvene the class and discuss:
  – Was it easy or difficult to paraphrase?
  – How did students feel when their partner paraphrased correctly what they had said?
  – Did it make them feel that their partner was listening intently?
  – Is paraphrasing merely parroting what has been said?
  – Would this be a useful technique for people in conflict?

## Extensions:
1 Conclude the paraphrasing exercise (Phase IV) with groups of 5–6 having a discussion. Each student has to paraphrase what the previous student has just said, to that person's satisfaction, before being allowed to contribute to the discussion.
2 In groups of 10+, students form a circle. One student whispers a sentence or a short story to the person on his right. Everyone has to pass this sentence or story around the circle accurately, word for word. Students are free to check with the previous speaker what he said, e.g. 'Is this what you said . . .?'
3 In pairs, students interview each other. Reconvene the class and invite each student to introduce his partner and tell the class what he has learnt about his partner. This reporting is to be checked for accuracy with the person being introduced.
4 Make a list of statements and ask the students to paraphrase them. This can be a written exercise and given as homework.
5 Make a list of 'feeling' statements. Students have to decide which feeling is reflected in the statement, e.g. 'My parents won't let me go to the disco on Saturday night. They're old fashioned and silly.' (The feeling is *anger* with the parents.)

## Notes:

The person who communicates effectively, is the person who hears accurately and reflects this back to the speaker in both verbal and non-verbal ways. This strategy introduces students to matching and paraphrasing. These are difficult skills to teach and the strategy is suitable for older, more able students.

'Matching', i.e. adopting body language which reflects that of the speaker, gives the speaker a feeling of being listened to and that the listener is 'in tune' with them. Students may find it awkward and somewhat artificial to copy another person's posture, hand movements and facial expressions. Watch for tendencies to exaggerate these movements. Really they should be a microscopic reflection of what the speaker is doing.

The second part of the strategy concentrates on hearing accurately and 'paraphrasing' what has been said. Again this can create harmony between speaker and listener when the listener reflects back accurately to the speaker what he has said. It is a communication skill which takes practice and time before becoming part of a person's communication repertoire. With more able students, this strategy could be extended to include the reflection of the speaker's feelings, so that feelings are paraphrased rather than content. This is a subtle communication skill which requires a lot of practice and expertise.

Skilful paraphrasing will require the students to reflect what the speaker has said in the student's own words. To repeat or echo your partner's words is to parrot rather than to paraphrase. Paraphrasing can be helped by phrases like: 'You feel . . .' 'It seems that . . .' 'You think . . .' and so on.

Further topics for discussion: 'My favourite TV programme', 'My idea of a perfect day', 'What I did over the weekend', 'If I had 24 hours to live'.

## Aim: To draw attention to behaviours that block communication.

# Procedure:

## ● Phase I

○ Invite the class to give examples of how people fail to listen in non-verbal ways.

○ Demonstrate with the help of a student a variety of these non-verbal, non-listening behaviours, e.g. yawning, looking at watch, fidgeting, no eye contact, bored expression, body turned away from speaker.

○ Form pairs and ask the students to decide who is to be A and B.

○ As talk to their partners on: 'If I had three wishes'.

○ Bs use a variety of non-verbal, non-listening behaviours.

○ After 1–2 minutes swap roles.

○ Reconvene the class and discuss:
   – How did it feel when they weren't listened to?
   – How did it feel when they weren't listening to their partners?
   – What happens in a relationship when people don't listen?

## ● Phase II

○ Explain to the class that there are communication breakdowns in the scenes about to be played.

○ The students are to analyse:
   – Why the communication is deficient.
   – What the communication block is.
   – How it could be avoided.

○ Two volunteers now dramatise the first communication-blocking script on the worksheet **NOT TUNED IN**. If necessary, they could repeat it.

○ Invite discussion on the following:
   – Was the communication good between the two people?
   – Why? Why not?
   – What was the communication block?
   – Which character created the block?
   – What effect did his/her behaviour have?
   – What effect would it have on them?
   – How would they feel about such a person?
   – How could the communication be better?

○ Continue in a similar way with the other communication-blocking scripts on the worksheet.

## Extensions:

1 Video record a dramatisation of the scripts and play it to the class in Phase II, instead of getting the students to read the scripts.

**Group Size:** Pairs

**Time:** 30–40 minutes

**Materials:** Readers require:

○ worksheet **NOT TUNED IN**

# Notes:

In the previous three strategies, students concentrated on the skills of listening and on the verbal and non-verbal ways of doing this. The course now progresses to consider ways we fail to listen, both verbal and non-verbal. This strategy looks at behaviours that block communication. In the next strategy, students will evaluate these blocking behaviours and assess themselves in the use of them.

Without realising it, many of us inject communication blocks into our conversations: we advise, interpret, and we make judgements. This can lead to feelings of resentment and defensiveness and the breakdown of communication.

This strategy focuses on four communication blocks: putting down, advising, interpreting and talking 'me me'. The teacher may wish to draw the students' attention to others: interrupting, ordering, threatening, moralising, probing, and so on.

Rather than use the four scripts in the one session, the teacher can spread their use over several sessions. The students who volunteer to read the scripts may require some time to prepare before they present them to the class. If necessary, the teacher could play the part of the 'blocker' to ensure that the block is interpreted correctly.

2 In small groups, students rewrite the scripts to become 'listening' scripts. The scenes are then replayed with the 'blocking' responses replaced by 'listening' ones.

3 Students complete sentences which focus on the communication blocks, e.g.
When someone interrupts my conversation I _____
When someone talks about themselves all the time I _____
The completed sentences are shared in small groups and the communication blocks discussed.

# NOT TUNED IN

## TALKING 'ME ME'

**Mark:** I'm really glad that term's over.

**Rajinder:** Yeah – I'm looking forward to the holiday, and I've been promised a new bike if I get a good report.

**Mark:** I'm dreading mine.

**Rajinder:** I know I've done well again. I'm sure I've come top in most subjects. I don't need to work hard. I know I'll get that bike.

**Mark:** It's my reading.

**Rajinder:** When I get that bike, I'm going to join the cycling club. The club is going on a touring holiday in France. I'll show you the photographs when I get back.

**Mark:** I try so hard.

**Rajinder:** Me – I don't need to work hard. I just do enough to get by. As my dad says, 'You've got it or you haven't'. I guess I've got it all!

## INTERPRETING

**Paul:** I'm going to help Dad with the car.

**Jane:** You're just trying to get Dad in a good mood so he'll let you stay out at the weekend.

**Paul:** No – I said I would help.

**Jane:** You're just creeping, just like you were yesterday with Mr Davies.

**Paul:** I stayed behind after school because I needed help with my work.

**Jane:** Oh yeah! Are you sure it wasn't to get out of walking the dog for Mum?

**Paul:** It was because Mr Davies offered to explain the work I missed last week.

**Jane:** You just wanted to make a good impression with the teachers. I know you.

**Paul:** I just want to do well in my exams.

## ADVISING

**Lyn:** I love your new dress. Wish I could afford a new one.

**Sue:** Why not? Just ask your mum.

**Lyn:** It's not that easy. I had a new blazer for school . . .

**Sue:** Yes it is – just tell her you need one for the school disco.

**Lyn:** I haven't asked if I may go yet!

**Sue:** You're silly – you just *tell* her you're going.

**Lyn:** Mum's usually OK but it's been difficult since Dad left.

**Sue:** That's your problem – you need to stand up for yourself. Just tell her you are going to the disco and you need a new dress.

## PUTTING DOWN

**Joan:** Viv?

**Viv:** Yes, four eyes, what is it this time?

**Joan:** Can you help me with my homework?

**Viv:** Sure, stupid. First give me a hand to move this table.

**Joan:** Just a second.

**Viv:** Hey, cloth ears! Did you hear me? I'd like this table *moved* some time before Christmas. Come on! Come on! Grab that end there.

**Joan:** Don't rush me.

**Viv:** OK – what's the problem?

**Joan:** It's my Maths. I don't understand what we did in class today.

**Viv:** That was easy. You must be dumb not to understand . . .

**Joan:** Anyhow, I haven't really got the time now.

**Viv:** It's OK . . . I'll ask someone else.

# Aim:
To help students evaluate the various communication blocks and to assess themselves in the use of these blocks.

# Procedure:

- **Phase I**
  - Give each student the worksheet **I'M NOT LISTENING**.
  - Students are free to add two communication blocks of their choice to the list.
  - Each student rank orders this list and enters the results in the PERSONAL column.
  - The greatest block to communication is ranked one.
  - Form pairs.
  - Each couple has to agree on the rank order or at least the first three.
  - The results are entered in the PAIRS column.
  - Pairs join to form groups of 4.
  - Again, each group has to agree on the rank order or at least the first three.
  - The results are entered in the FOURS column.
  - This is repeated in groups of 8.
  - Reconvene the class and discuss:
    - Which was felt to be the greatest block to communication?
    - Why?
    - Are students conscious that they use communication blocks?

- **Phase II**
  - Form groups of 4–6.
  - Give each student the worksheet **DO I LISTEN?**
  - Each group decides on a focal person.
  - The focal person invites each group member in turn to:
    (a) comment on his PUTTING DOWN behaviours, and
    (b) say which box on the assessment sheet they would tick for him, i.e. very often/fairly often/sometimes, etc.
  - After listening to what the group members have said, the focal person ticks a box on the assessment sheet which he feels is correct for him.
  - Students take it in turn to be the focal person and work through the list of communication blocks.
  - Students now complete the remaining section of the worksheet.

### Extension:
The assessment exercise can be carried out privately, with students completing their worksheets on their own, or with a partner of their choice.

**Group Size:** Pyramid groupings; 4–6

**Time:** 30–40 minutes

**Materials:** Each student requires:
- worksheet **I'M NOT LISTENING**
- worksheet **DO I LISTEN?**

# Notes:

This exercise, which is a follow-on from the previous strategy, invites students to evaluate common communication blocks and to assess themselves on these.

The rank-ordering activity will provide opportunity for discussion and for students to examine the outcomes of the various communication blocks. Encourage students to justify why they have made particular choices. Agreement over the rank ordering is more likely to be reached if students listen to and become aware of each other's perspectives.

Some students may feel uncomfortable during the assessment in Phase II, and the teacher will need to be vigilant of and sensitive to students who may feel vulnerable.

The teacher may wish to make the assessment a private exercise and follow the suggestion in the Extension. It could be given as a homework assignment, where students can invite parents or friends to assess them on those behaviours.

# I'M NOT LISTENING

Name _____

Date _____

Add two communication blocks to this list.

RIDICULING

CRITICISING

PREACHING

| | Personal | Pairs | Fours | Eights |
|---|---|---|---|---|
| **PUTTING DOWN**<br>(makes others feel bad and<br>inadequate . . . likes to hurt) | | | | |
| **INTERPRETING**<br>(makes judgements about<br>what others say and do) | | | | |
| **TALKING 'ME ME'**<br>(likes to talk about him or<br>herself all the time . . . no<br>real interest in others) | | | | |
| **ADVISING**<br>(likes to tell people what to<br>do and how to do it . . . 'I<br>know best' mentality) | | | | |
| **INTERRUPTING**<br>(cuts across in conversation<br>. . . little regard for the<br>person speaking) | | | | |
| | | | | |
| | | | | |

Rank these communication blocks. The greatest block to communication scores 1.

JUDGING

AGGRESSIVE

BLAMING

DOMINATING

THREATENING

# DO I LISTEN?

INTERRUPTING

ME ME ME ME

Name _____

Date _____

Add two communication blocks to this list.

| | Very often | Fairly often | Sometimes | Not often | Never |
|---|---|---|---|---|---|
| **PUTTING DOWN** (makes others feel bad and inadequate . . . likes to hurt) | | | | | |
| **INTERPRETING** (makes judgements about what others say and do) | | | | | |
| **TALKING 'ME ME'** (likes to talk about him or herself all the time . . . no real interest in others) | | | | | |
| **ADVISING** (likes to tell people what to do and how to do it . . . 'I know best' mentality) | | | | | |
| **INTERRUPTING** (cuts across in conversation . . . little regard for the person speaking) | | | | | |
| | | | | | |
| | | | | | |

A communication block I seldom use is: _____

A communication block I use frequently is: _____

35

**Aim:** To help students appraise their interpersonal communication skills.

## Procedure:

○ Form pairs and students decide who is to be A and B.
  – A takes part in the discussion/task.
  – B observes A's communication skills.
○ Give the observer's sheet **HOW DO I RATE?** to B.
○ Draw attention to the behaviours to be observed and explain how the sheet is to be completed.
○ As gather together in groups of 6–8.
○ Each group forms a circle – an inner circle.
○ Bs form a circle around them.
○ Each B is to sit opposite her partner so that she can see her clearly.
○ As have 8–10 minutes to complete their task:

> You are the only survivors from a shipwreck. You are marooned on a remote island. You are to decide on six laws to live by.

○ Swap roles and repeat the procedure.
○ Regroup to the original pairs.
○ Allow time for students to complete any unfinished sections of the observer's sheet.
○ Students take it in turn to give feedback to their partners on the communication skills observed and hand them the observation sheets.

### Extension:
Video record the group discussion/task and play this back to the group. This enables students to observe and assess themselves. It also allows the teacher to draw attention to specific behaviours.

**Group Size:** Pairs; 6–8

**Time:** 30–40 minutes

**Materials:** Each student requires:

○ observer's sheet **HOW DO I RATE?**

## Notes:

This strategy allows students to practise the communication skills which have been taught during the course and to receive some feedback on their use of these skills.

Encourage students to complete the COMMENTS section of the observer's sheet, e.g.

| Does she or he: | YES/NO | HOW OFTEN? | COMMENTS |
|---|---|---|---|
| join in | yes | 11 | appeared hesitant |
| fidget | yes | 1111 | scratched his ears |

Instead of using the island task, assessment could be carried out in groups of four: two speakers and two observers, who rotate roles after the speakers have engaged in a brief discussion. However, although suitable in some contexts, this procedure can prove artificial and a small group of 6–8 students in discussion is generally more successful. Here are some topics which could be used for discussion: 'Boys are stronger than girls', 'The school uniform', 'Boys don't understand girls', 'School meals', 'Drugs', 'Good looks are more important than personality'.

The worksheet **TASKS**, that follows, suggests some activities which could be used as alternatives to the 'remote island' task described in the Procedure.

# HOW DO I RATE?

Name _____

Observed by _____

Date _____

**Does she or he:**

| | YES/NO | HOW OFTEN? | COMMENTS |
|---|---|---|---|
| join in | | | |
| speak clearly | | | |
| listen | | | |
| fidget | | | |
| use gestures | | | |
| interrupt | | | |
| look at the person speaking | | | |
| ask questions | | | |
| use put-downs | | | |

**CIRCLE THOSE WORDS WHICH APPLY:**

anxious    co-operative    cheerful

friendly    interested    embarrassed

nervous    relaxed    uptight

helpful    bored    confident

Skill that is used very well ...............

Skill that requires more practice ...............

Overall score ............... /10

---

# HOW DO I RATE?

Name _____

Observed by _____

Date _____

**Does she or he:**

| | YES/NO | HOW OFTEN? | COMMENTS |
|---|---|---|---|
| join in | | | |
| speak clearly | | | |
| listen | | | |
| fidget | | | |
| use gestures | | | |
| interrupt | | | |
| look at the person speaking | | | |
| ask questions | | | |
| use put-downs | | | |

**CIRCLE THOSE WORDS WHICH APPLY:**

anxious    co-operative    cheerful

friendly    interested    embarrassed

nervous    relaxed    uptight

helpful    bored    confident

Skill that is used very well ...............

Skill that requires more practice ...............

Overall score ............... /10

# TASKS

---

## DESERT SURVIVAL

**Materials: None**                    **Time: 10–15 mins.**                    **Group Size: 4–6**

IMAGINE YOUR PLANE HAS CRASH-LANDED IN THE DESERT. THERE ARE NO SURVIVORS
EXCEPT THIS GROUP. ALL AROUND YOU IS FLAT DESERT AND THE TEMPERATURE IS ALREADY
100°F. RANK IN ORDER OF IMPORTANCE FOR YOUR SURVIVAL THE ITEMS LISTED HERE:

| | |
|---|---|
| Magnetic compass | Loaded pistol |
| Jack-knife | Torch |
| Cosmetic mirror | Bottle of salt tablets |
| Quart of water | 1 box of powdered milk |
| First-aid kit | A brightly coloured parachute |

---

## PINS AND STRAWS

**Materials: Lots of pins and straws**        **Time: 10–15 mins.**        **Group Size: 4–6**

YOU HAVE 10–15 MINUTES TO DESIGN AND BUILD A STRUCTURE USING ONLY PINS AND
STRAWS. AT THE END EACH STRUCTURE WILL BE JUDGED FOR ITS HEIGHT, STABILITY AND
UNUSUAL SHAPE.
BEFORE BUILDING, SPEND SOME TIME TALKING ABOUT THE DESIGN AND HOW PEOPLE ARE
GOING TO WORK TO ACHIEVE THIS.

---

## HOLIDAY

**Materials: None**                    **Time: 10–15 mins.**                    **Group Size: 4–6**

YOU ARE ON A YOUTH CLUB CAMPING HOLIDAY. AS THE MINIBUS ARRIVES AT THE
CAMPSITE, THE YOUTH LEADER COLLAPSES AND IS RUSHED TO HOSPITAL SUFFERING FROM
APPENDICITIS. THE GROUP DECIDES TO CONTINUE WITH THE HOLIDAY. THE EQUIPMENT
(TENTS, COOKERS, ETC.) HAS NOT YET BEEN UNPACKED AND THE CAMP SHOP CLOSES IN
30 MINUTES.

THE GROUP IS TO DECIDE ON:
– a list of jobs that need to be done.
– who is to do these jobs.
– outings during the day or evening for the week.

**Aim:** To help students identify target behaviours and commit themselves to these using a structured plan for behaviour change.

# Procedure:

## • Phase I
○ Give each student the worksheet **MY COMMUNICATION SKILLS**.
○ Using the results of the previous assessment work, students complete this worksheet.
○ Students are free to work individually, with a partner of their choice or in small groups.
○ Form groups of 4–5.
○ Students take it in turn to share Part Two of the completed worksheet.
○ Students are free to pass.

## • Phase II
○ Each student decides on a priority goal he wishes to work on.
○ Explain the elements of successful goal achievement (see Notes).
○ Give each student the worksheets **A SELF CONTRACT** and **SUCCESS!**
○ Comment on the worksheets saying how and when they are to be completed.
○ Students may work on their own, with a partner of their choice or in small groups.
○ Allow time for students to fill in the worksheet **A SELF CONTRACT**.
○ Students may ask for ideas and support from other group members in achieving their goal.
○ Set a future date for students to review and share progress.
○ When students have achieved their goal they complete the worksheet **SUCCESS!**

## Extensions:
1 Students invite people of their choice to assess their use of the skills listed on the worksheet **MY COMMUNICATION SKILLS**. A balanced assessment is more likely to be achieved by asking four contrasting people, e.g. parent, teacher, friend and brother or sister.
2 Students use a copy of the grid opposite to identify people they find it difficult to communicate with. A plan of action for communicating more effectively with these people could then be drawn up using the worksheet **A SELF CONTRACT**.

**Group Size:** Varies; 4–5

**Time:** 30–40 minutes

**Materials:** Each student requires:
○ worksheet **MY COMMUNICATION SKILLS**
○ worksheet **A SELF CONTRACT**
○ worksheet **SUCCESS!**
○ completed assessment/observers' sheets from strategies 5, 6, 9 and 10

| I COMMUN-ICATE EASILY | with MUM | DAD | BROTHER | SISTER | GRANDPARENTS | AUNTS/UNCLES | BOY/GIRLFRIEND | NEIGHBOURS | MALE FRIENDS | FEMALE FRIENDS | SHOP ASSISTANTS | TEACHERS |
|---|---|---|---|---|---|---|---|---|---|---|---|---|
| Very often | | | | | | | | | | | | |
| Fairly often | | | | | | | | | | | | |
| Sometimes | | | | | | | | | | | | |
| Not often | | | | | | | | | | | | |
| Never | | | | | | | | | | | | |

I wish I could communicate more effectively with:

1 _____   2 _____

3 In groups of 4–6, students take it in turn to offer a goal for the group's consideration. The group brainstorms for ideas on how to achieve this goal and the student uses these ideas to complete **A SELF CONTRACT** worksheet.
4 Students write a goal on a slip of paper. These are folded and handed to the teacher who mixes them and selects one at random. The class brainstorms for ideas on how to achieve this goal. In this way, students can get ideas and help without revealing their identities.
5 In small groups, each student writes his goal on a sheet of paper. This is passed to the person on the right who writes suggestions for achieving this goal on the bottom of the sheet. This is folded over and passed to the next person on the right. This continues until each student has his original sheet again. The student now uses these ideas in deciding on a plan for goal achievement.
6 Create time at the beginning of the next few sessions for students to review their goals and the plans for achieving them.

# Notes:

Students at this stage in the course have not only identified the skills of interpersonal communication and practised them but have also received feedback on their use of these skills. This strategy provides students with the opportunity to decide on the communication skills they would like to improve on and draw up a plan of action for achieving this.

This is not a negative exercise but a moment to highlight those communication skills the student is good at, as well as drawing attention to those requiring attention.

The following five stages provide a structure for successful goal achievement:

(a) *Goal:* Warn against the goal being set too high. It is to be realistic and attainable. The goal: 'I'm going to be a better communicator' is too vague to be of much value. 'I am going to improve my eye contact' has more meaning as a goal.

(b) *Plan:* The steps to achieving the goal are to be practical and workable, e.g.

(i) I am going to practise looking at my own eyes in the mirror.

(ii) I shall practise looking into my friend's eyes, holding contact for three seconds and gradually increasing the time.

(iii) I shall try to carry out a conversation with my friend and keep eye contact.

(iv) When I am ready, I shall try this with others and ask my friend to observe me. (If this is too difficult, I shall look at a spot on the other person's forehead.)

(c) *Support system:* Who is going to help the student achieve the goal? What part can peers, home, staff play? These people are to be consulted if they are to support the student. 'I shall ask my best friend to help me.'

(d) *Time:* A realistic time should be set for the goal to be achieved, which will vary from person to person, e.g. 'I shall start tonight and hope by the end of the month to be able to keep eye contact with people.'

(e) *Celebration:* The student rewards himself when the goal has been achieved, e.g. 'My friend and I will celebrate by going to the ice-rink.'

Some long-term goals may require several short-term goals to be realised first, so make the **A SELF CONTRACT** and **SUCCESS!** worksheets available to students as and when necessary.

Goal setting should not be seen as a one-off moment but as a continuous process with students monitoring their own and each other's progress, reviewing goals, plans and support systems.

# MY COMMUNICATION SKILLS

Name _____   Date _____

## Part One

| Do I | Very often | Often | Sometimes | Not often | Never |
|------|------------|-------|-----------|-----------|-------|
| interrupt? | | | | | |
| fidget? | | | | | |
| consider other's feelings? | | | | | |
| giggle nervously? | | | | | |
| show interest in the person speaking? | | | | | |
| note people's body language? | | | | | |
| consider people's points of view? | | | | | |
| use put-downs? | | | | | |
| keep eye contact? | | | | | |
| show interest in what is being talked about? | | | | | |
| talk a lot about myself? | | | | | |
| use gestures? | | | | | |
| respect people's personal space? | | | | | |
| encourage others to keep talking? | | | | | |

## Part Two

DO I GIGGLE NERVOUSLY?

The communication skills I use best are:

_____
_____

_____
_____

DO I USE GESTURES?

The communication skills I could improve on are:

_____
_____

_____
_____

## My priority goals are:

1 _____

2 _____

# A SELF CONTRACT

I : _____ PROMISE THAT BY : _____
      (YOUR FULL NAME)                                    (DATE TO BE ACHIEVED)

I WILL : _____
                                                   (YOUR GOAL)

BY DOING : 1 _____
           2 _____
           3 _____
                                                   (YOUR PLAN)

WITH THE HELP OF : _____
                                                   (YOUR SUPPORT)

AND WILL CELEBRATE BY :
         _____
                                         (DETAILS OF CELEBRATION)


SIGNED : _____   DATE : _____
            (YOUR SIGNATURE)              (TODAY'S DATE)

WITNESSED BY
_____
(SIGNATURE OF WITNESS)

DATE _____

# SUCCESS!

Name _____

## Aim:
To provide an opportunity for fun, assessment and practice in the skills of interpersonal communication.

## Procedure:

### • Phase I

○ Form groups of 5–6.
○ Give each group a set of **GAME TALK CARDS** and a set of **PARTNER CARDS**.
○ Explain the game and set a time limit.
○ Each player is to select a **GAME TALK** and a **PARTNER** card.
○ The **GAME TALK** card sets the task.
○ The **PARTNER** card determines the player's partner for the task.
○ The cards are shuffled, placed face down in two piles and each group decides who will start.
○ This person selects the top card from both piles, completes the task with her partner and returns the cards to the bottom of the piles.
○ Students take it in turn to play.

### • Phase II

○ Reconvene the class and discuss:
  – Did students enjoy the game?
  – Which tasks were easy?
  – Which tasks were difficult?
  – What have we learned/been reminded of in playing the game?
  – How can these skills become part of our everyday style of communication?

## Extension:
Invite students to design a game on Interpersonal Communication. It may be a board game, card game or a computer game, and should reflect the skills identified and taught during this course. The teacher could offer prizes for the best designs.

**Group Size:** 5–6

**Time:** No fixed time

**Materials:** Each group requires:
○ set of **GAME TALK CARDS**
○ set of **PARTNER CARDS**

## Notes:

This game focuses on the skills that have been highlighted during the course and provides an opportunity for fun, assessment, renewed awareness and practice in these skills.

It works best towards the end of the course on **INTERPERSONAL COMMUNICATION**, as the game presupposes some skills with non-verbal behaviours, open-ended questioning, and so on.

The cards will look more attractive if reproduced on coloured card, preferably a different colour for the **GAME TALK** and **PARTNER** cards. A set of cards for every 5–6 players is usually best, though the game can be played with more or fewer players.

The game should be played at a brisk pace allowing all students the opportunity to participate.

# GAME TALK CARDS

**You and your partner answer this question:**

Who in the group probably finds it easiest to meet new people?

---

**Ask your partner:**

What words do open-ended questions usually begin with? Name two.

Ans. What/How/When/Where

---

**You and your partner answer this question:**

Who in the group is most relaxed and friendly when talking to others?

---

Ask the group to assume a body position which signals *boredom*.

**Your partner decides which is best and why.**

---

On a scale of 1–10, how good are you at starting a conversation with someone you don't know?

**Ask your partner to rate you.**

---

**Ask your partner:**

In a conversation what amount of time is spent keeping eye contact — a third, a half, two-thirds?

Ans. about one-third

---

Take up a body position which matches your partner's.

---

**You and your partner complete this sentence:**

The people I find it difficult to speak to are _____

---

**You and your partner answer this question:**

Who in the group is most likely to consider other people's feelings?

---

Your partner is to talk for 30 seconds about him/herself. You are to paraphrase what he/she has said.

---

On a scale of 1–10, how good are you at considering other people's feelings?

**Ask your partner to rate you.**

---

Talk for 30 seconds about everything you did since getting up this morning.

**Your partner is to make 3 comments about your communication skills.**

---

**You and your partner complete this sentence:**

When someone interrupts me I _____

---

**You and your partner complete this sentence:**

When someone listens to me I feel _____

---

On a scale of 1–10, how often do you interrupt?

**Ask your partner to rate you.**

---

**You and your partner answer this question:**

Who in the group has good eye contact?

# GAME TALK CARDS

Think of a famous personality.

**Your partner has one minute to find out who it is by asking open-ended questions only.**

---

**Ask your partner:**

What tips would you give to someone who finds eye contact difficult?

*Check this answer with the group.*

---

**Ask your partner:**

Who in the group is good at noting people's body language?

---

**Ask your partner:**

Who in the group listens carefully and attentively?

---

Speak about yourself for 30 seconds.

**Your partner is to mirror your body language.**

---

**Ask your partner:**

What is the secret of being considered a good conversationalist?

*Check this answer with the group.*

---

Interview your partner, asking three open-ended questions.

---

**Ask your partner:**

What tips would you give to someone who finds it difficult to keep a conversation going?

*Check this answer with the group.*

---

Ans. 14,000

**Ask your partner:**

About how many words has the average 6-year-old mastered:
5,000/10,000/14,000?

---

**Ask your partner:**

Who in the group is good at encouraging others to talk?

---

On a scale of 1–10, how shy are you?

**Ask your partner to rate you.**

---

On a scale of 1–10, how much do you fidget?

**Ask your partner to rate you.**

---

**Ask your partner:**

Why were we born with two ears but only one mouth (according to a Greek philosopher)?

Ans. So that we may listen twice as much as we talk.

---

Describe your partner's body language and the messages he/she is giving.

---

On a scale of 1–10, how good is your eye contact?

**Ask your partner to rate you.**

---

How confident are you when talking to the opposite sex?

**Ask your partner to rate him/herself on a scale of 1–10.**

# GAME TALK CARDS

On a scale of 1–10, how clear and interesting does your voice sound?

**Ask your partner to rate you.**

---

**Ask your partner:**

Which player is most likely to involve the quieter members in a group discussion?

---

Talk about yourself for one minute. Your partner is to stand behind you and supply the hand movements.

---

**Ask your partner:**

In a conversation, who keeps the most eye contact — the person speaking or the person listening?

Ans. The person listening usually looks at the speaker most of the time.

---

**Ask your partner:**

List three ways that people show they are failing to listen.

*Check these answers with the group.*

---

**Ask your partner:**

What is the world record for non-stop talking?

Ans. 240 hours.

---

Your partner is to speak about him/herself for one minute. You are constantly to interrupt. At the end, check out your partner's feelings.

---

**Ask your partner:**

How much of our communication is non-verbal: less than 40%/ between 40% and 60%/ more than 60%?

Ans. Some psychologists suggest it is 70–80%.

---

'Sculpt' your partner into a listening pose.

---

**Ask your partner:**

Who in the group do you enjoy talking to the most? Why?

---

On a scale of 1–10, how good a listener are you?

**Ask your partner to rate you.**

---

**Ask your partner to give two reasons why people might find you easy to get on with.**

---

Talk for 30 seconds about your partner's strengths, achievements and successes.

**Each group member is now to make one comment on your communication skills.**

---

**You and your partner complete this sentence:**

The people I find it easy to speak to are _____

---

On a scale of 1–10, how much do you encourage others to talk?

**Ask your partner to rate you.**

---

In what ways do you fidget?

**Ask your partner to answer this question about you.**

---

# GAME TALK CARDS

'Sculpt' your partner into a body position which communicates *anger*.

Say two things about your partner's style of communication.

**Ask your partner:**
Who in the group is most likely to consider other people's points of view?

On a scale of 1–10, how often do you give put-downs?
**Ask your partner to rate you.**

---

Interview your partner, asking three YES/NO type questions.

**Ask your partner:**
What tips would you give to someone who finds meeting new people difficult?
*Check this answer with the group.*

**Ask your partner:**
Who in the group is best at making other people feel important and listened to?

On a scale of 1–10, how good are you at respecting other people's personal space?
**Ask your partner to rate you.**

---

**Ask your partner:**
Who in the group is likely to check every now and again to make sure they understand what is being said?

**Ask your partner:**
Who in the group has the most interesting-sounding voice, i.e. one which isn't dull, flat or boring?

**Ask your partner:**
What does the following mean: People hearing without listening; people talking without speaking?
*Check this answer with the group.*

**You and your partner complete this sentence:**
A communication skill I would like to be better at is ____

---

**Ask your partner:**
In a day, what percentage of time does the average person spend (a) listening? (b) talking?

Ans. listening 42% talking 32%

**Ask your partner:**
List 3 ways that people show they are listening attentively.
*Check this answer with the group.*

Think of a famous personality.
**Your partner has one minute to find out who it is by asking YES/NO questions only.**

Ask the group to assume a body language which signals *no emotion* whatsoever.
**Your partner decides which is best.**

# PARTNER CARDS

| | | | |
|---|---|---|---|
| A PERSON WITH DARK HAIR | THE THIRD PERSON ON YOUR RIGHT | A PERSON WITH BLUE EYES | THE THIRD PERSON ON YOUR LEFT |
| A PERSON WHO LIKES MATHS | A PERSON WITH FAIR HAIR | THE SECOND PERSON ON YOUR RIGHT | THE OLDEST PERSON |
| THE YOUNGEST PERSON | A PERSON WHO LIKES SPORT | A PERSON WITH BROWN EYES | THE PERSON ON YOUR LEFT |
| THE PERSON ON YOUR RIGHT | THE TALLEST PERSON | THE PERSON OPPOSITE YOU | THE SECOND PERSON ON YOUR LEFT |

# HOW HAVE WE GOT ON? ■■ ■ ■

**Aim:** To review the course on **INTERPERSONAL COMMUNICATION** and to assess the student's response to it.

## Procedure:

- **Phase I**
  - ○ Divide the class into two circles, an inner and an outer circle, with the students facing each other in pairs.
  - ○ Tell the students to discuss: 'What I liked about this course' with their partners.
  - ○ Allow 2–3 minutes for this.
  - ○ Inner circle moves to the left and students now discuss: 'What I disliked about this course'.
  - ○ Continue this procedure with the following discussion topics:
    - – Why I enjoyed/didn't enjoy this course.
    - – Suggestions I have for improving the course.
    - – The most important thing I have learnt probably is . . .
    - – What I consider important in communicating with others is . . .
    - – I am good at communicating with others because . . .

- **Phase II**
  - ○ Give each student the worksheet **HOW HAVE I GOT ON?**
  - ○ Comment as necessary.
  - ○ Students are to complete these working individually.
  - ○ The completed sheets are collected and handed to the teacher.

### Extensions:

1 Turn the phrases on the worksheet into questions, e.g. 'Did you enjoy the course – a lot? a bit? not at all?' etc. and write each question on a large sheet of paper. Display these around the room. Students are to wander around the room answering the questions by writing on the sheets of paper. Conclude by commenting on each sheet and inviting further comments.

2 Students complete and share a list of incomplete sentences which will help them review the course, e.g. 'I liked this course because . . .', 'I am pleased I did . . .', 'I would like to do more of . . .', 'I learned . . .'.

**Group Size:** Varies

**Time:** 30–40 minutes

**Materials:** Each student requires:
- ○ worksheet **HOW HAVE I GOT ON?**

## Notes:

Evaluation is an essential function in any education programme. It enables teachers to monitor progress and provides them with feedback on the effectiveness of the programme, course materials and strategies. Ideally evaluation should be regarded as a continuous process and not an isolated procedure tackled at the end of a course.

Young people are inclined to find evaluation difficult and a written questionnaire often gets limited results. So Phase I begins with an activity intended to stimulate students' memories, feelings and judgement. This is then followed by the questionnaire.

# HOW HAVE I GOT ON ?

Name _____     Date _____

I have found this course useful:

very └─┴─┴─┴─┴─┘ not at all

I have enjoyed this course:

a lot └─┴─┴─┴─┴─┘ not at all

## CIRCLE THE WORDS YOU FEEL APPLY TO THE COURSE:

confusing        irrelevant        stressful        stimulating        relevant

disappointing

depressing

easy        fun                                           interesting

difficult        boring        relaxing        entertaining

helpful

Two things I disliked about the course:

1 ........................................

2 ........................................

Two things I liked about the course:

1 ........................................

2 ........................................

Rate the following:

worksheets   very useful └─┴─┴─┴─┴─┘ not at all

discussion           └─┴─┴─┴─┴─┘

teacher talking      └─┴─┴─┴─┴─┘

video (if used)      └─┴─┴─┴─┴─┘

role-play            └─┴─┴─┴─┴─┘

Probably the most important thing
I have learnt is:

........................................

........................................

My suggestions for improving the course are:

........................................

........................................

## WHAT I CONSIDER TO BE IMPORTANT IN COMMUNICATING WITH OTHERS IS:

...................................................................

...................................................................

...................................................................

The goals I have set myself are:

........................................

........................................

I am good at communicating with others because:

........................................

........................................

Video can be a useful teaching aid in a course on interpersonal communication. It provides an opportunity for students to become aware of how others see them. It can be used:
• as a self-awareness tool
• for modelling behaviours
• to provide objective feedback when experimenting with new behaviours
• to show educational programmes on body language, etc.

Students may feel vulnerable when 'exposed' to video and the teacher will need to be sensitive to this. Students will generally feel less under pressure in small group work rather than in pair work. A horseshoe formation, with the camera set back to include everyone, works well and does not require an operator. It also provides an opportunity for the teacher to join in if appropriate. Set the monitor screen so that it cannot be seen by the group being recorded and reassure them that the recordings will not be shown to other groups. Any initial showing-off in front of the camera usually disappears when the novelty wears off.

Playback can be used in the following ways:
• for general, overall self-assessment
• to focus on specific behaviour, e.g. eye contact
• to focus on individual performances.
It is best if the teacher directs students' attention to specific behaviours during the playback, helping them to evaluate their behaviour, and asking questions such as, 'Are you happy with that?' 'Are those the messages you want to convey?' 'Would you want to do it differently now?' 'How?' and so on. In this way, the student, not the teacher, is making decisions about which behaviour, if any, needs to change. During the playback, students could assess themselves using the worksheets from this course or could create their own checklists.